SQUADRONS!

No. 51

The Last of the Long-Range Biplane Flying Boats

Phil H. Listemann

ISBN: 979-1096490-86-8

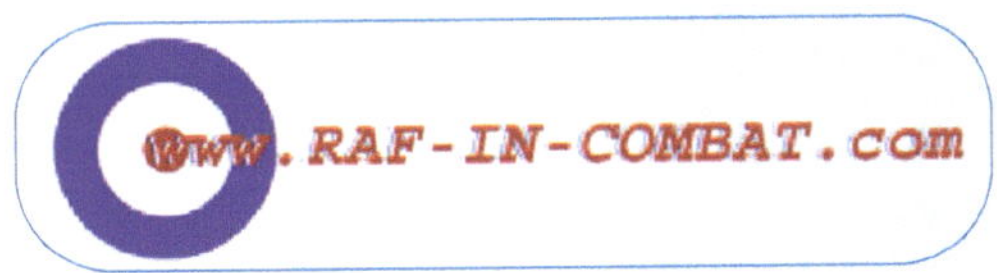

Colour profiles: Bill Dady/Claveworks-graphics

Glossary of Terms

Personel :

(AUS)/RAF: Australian serving in the RAF
(BEL)/RAF: Belgian serving in the RAF
(CAN)/RAF: Canadian serving in the RAF
(CZ)/RAF: Czechoslovak serving in the RAF
(NFL)/RAF: Newfoundlander serving in the RAF
(NL)/RAF: Dutch serving in the RAF
(NZ)/RAF: New Zealander serving in the RAF
(POL)/RAF: Pole serving in the RAF
(SR)/RAF: Rhodesian serving in the RAF
(SA)/RAF: South African serving in the RAF
(US)/RAF - RCAF : American serving in the RAF or RCAF

Ranks

G/C : Group Captain
W/C : Wing Commander
S/L : Squadron Leader
F/L : Flight Lieutenant
F/O : Flying Officer
P/O : Pilot Officer
W/O : Warrant Officer
F/Sgt : Flight Sergeant
Sgt : Sergeant
Cpl : Corporal
LAC : Leading Aircraftman

Other

ATA: Air Transport Auxiliary
CO : Commander
DFC : Distinguished Flying Cross
DFM : Distinguished Flying Medal
DSO : Distinguished Service Order
Eva. : Evaded
ORB : Operational Record Book
OTU : Operational Training Unit
PoW : Prisoner of War
PAF: Polish Air Force
RAF : Royal Air Force
RAAF : Royal Australian Air Force
RCAF : Royal Canadian Air Force
RNZAF : Royal New Zealand Air Force
SAAF : South African Air Force
s/d: Shot down
Sqn : Squadron
† : Killed

The Blackburn Iris

In the years following the end of WWI, the RAF maintained a small number of flying boats in place of the numerous squadrons that ringed the British Isles and were distributed throughout the Mediterranean. The need for convoy escorts had resulted in a major expansion in the requirements for flying boats, seaplanes and landplanes. Coupled with this was the rapid progress in the development of anti-submarine equipment, mainly in the form of special bombs, but also including detection gear, even though the latter device could only be used by landing the aircraft on the surface and listening though hydrophones but both flying boats and seaplanes were fitted with these for trials before the end of WWI.

The Air Ministry produced a variety of specifications for reconnaissance flying boats to replace the wartime F.5, which itself was updated and rebuilt in service. Specification 9/23 was for a three-engine long-range machine, the initial draft being replaced by 14/24. This produced the Blackburn Iris I; one prototype (**N185**) was ordered which first flew in June 1926, powered by three 650-hp Rolls-Royce Condor III engines, and featuring a wooden hull and mixed construction wings. However, soakage of the wooden hull degraded performance and it was decided in March 1927 to rebuild N185 with a metal hull. More powerful engines were also installed, 675-hp Rolls-Royce Condor IIIAs, and the new N185, now with the denomination of Iris Mk.II, flew again on 2 August 1927. Tested, the Iris II performed well, and it was found the type was worth developing, so a specification was drawn up for an improved version, the Iris III. Differing mainly in that the wings were built of duralumin with a fabric covering, the prototype, **N238**, first flew on 21 November 1929. As subsequent testing was satisfactory, an order for two Iris IIIs was placed (**S1263** and **S1264**), followed by a replacement airframe, **S1593**, after the loss of N238. The Iris III was armed with three 0.303-in machine guns, one mounted forward and two aft in open cockpits, and the normal crew was five. Up to 2,000lb of bombs could be carried. Other developments led to the Iris IV, after converting N185 to three 800-hp Armstrong Siddeley Leopard III radial engines, but this configuration never saw service, and the Iris V fitted with 825-hp Rolls-Royce Buzzard IIMS engines with larger propellers. There was no prototype of the Iris V as all were Iris III conversions: S1263 in March 1932; S1264 in January 1933; and S1593 in March 1933. S1264 never returned to service as it sank at its mooring during a night-time gale off Felixstowe very shortly after its conversion. By June 1934, only one Iris survived, S1593, but it continued to fly as a manufacturer's testbed until April 1938. It never flew again but was consigned to testing anti-corrosive paints for a little while longer.

Into service

To operate the Iris, No. 209 Squadron was formed at Mount Batten on 15 March 1930. On 5 February, S1263 arrived and was supplemented by N238 on 15 May, even though the latter required extensive repairs and was not taken into service until 30 September. On 4 June, S1264 arrived. The trio was soon split up when, on 4 February 1931, N238 flew into the water on approach at 70 mph and broke up after it nose-dived. Nine of the crew perished, the other three were injured. A replacement Iris III, S1593, was taken on charge in July 1931. In June 1932, S1263 returned to 209 Squadron but, on 12 January 1933, the flying boat collided with a pinnace and sank while landing, causing the death of one crewmember and leaving 209 without an Iris until S1593 re-joined in March. It continued to serve until April 1934 when the Blackburn Perth became available.

Iris I N185, with a metal hull, landing off Felixstowe.

Above: Iris III N238, with Condor IIIA engines, on the ramp at Felixstowe.
Below: Iris V S1263 wearing a stylised 209 Squadron badge between the nose gunner's position and the cockpit.

Above: Iris V S1263 of 209 Squadron flying along the Cornish coast.
Below: Iris III S1593 before its delivery to 209 Squadron.

The Blackburn Perth

The development of the Iris didn't stop with the Mk.V. An improved version, the Mk.VI was designed but used the same engines and was actually not much different to the Mk.V. The beam was slightly increased to improve buoyancy and the pilots sat in an enclosed cockpit. Other minor improvements were also included. Three flying boats were ordered as **K3580–K3582** and delivered between December 1933 and January 1934. The change of name to Perth was probably for the best given the various setbacks the Iris suffered during its career. A fourth Perth, **K4011**, was later ordered and delivered in April 1934 but would only serve for experimental purposes until being struck off charge in February 1938.

Into service

The three Perths of the first contract also served with No. 209 Squadron. The first to reach the squadron was K3581 in January 1934, followed by K3182 the following month. K3180 was taken on charge by 209 in May. The career of the Perth was plagued with various groundings due to issues with the tail units which started during the autumn of 1934. These eventually forced the removal of the tail units, for delivery to Blackburn in March 1935, effectively leaving 209 without a Perth for the next four months; the flying boats were eventually back at the squadron in July. To fill the gap, 209 acquired the London and Stranraer prototypes as well as the Short R.24/31. Trouble continued as, on 14 September, K3580 lost a float on take-off in heavy seas at Stornoway and crashed. While there were no casualties, the aircraft was too damaged for economical repair. The remaining two Perths continued to serve until January 1936, shortly before the arrival of the Short Singapore, which at the time had already proven to be a more practical flying boat. They were struck off charge soon after even though K3581 was passed to the Marine Aircraft Experimental Establishment (MAEE) for research purposes, including investigating mooring and slipping equipment.

Perth K3582 with 209 Squadron's badge below the cockpit. Except for the cockpit canopy, there were few obvious differences between the Iris and the Perth. The change of name was more symbolic than a need to obey RAF regulations regarding the name given to its aircraft.

Above: Perth K4011 on a routine patrol.
Below: Perth K3581 after its decommissioning when it was used to test mooring equipment.

The Short Rangoon

The Short Rangoon was the military version of the Short Calcutta, the latter intended to serve with Imperial Airways. It was a large flying boat with three engines capable of carrying fifteen passengers and mail over the Empire air routes. Shorts used the airframe to conform with Specification R.18/29, calling for a replacement of No. 203 Squadron's Southamptons operating in the Persian Gulf. The conversion was relatively straightforward as the design was based on the Calcutta built for the French Navy; no prototype was required. Therefore, in 1930, three examples were ordered as Short Rangoons and given serials **S1433**, **S1434** and **S1435**. Flying with a crew of five, they were powered by three 540-hp Bristol Jupiter XIF radial engines, defended by three machine guns in the nose and two dorsal positions, and capable of carrying a bomb load of 1,000lb. They made their first flights respectively on 24 September, 2 December and 20 December 1930.

The Air Ministry ordered three more Rangoons in the following years: **K2134** delivered in February 1932; **K2809** in November 1932; and **K3678** in May 1934.

Into service

Once tested, the first three Rangoons were issued to 203 Squadron at Felixstowe in January 1931. The following month, the flying boats left for the Middle East with G/C W.L. Welsh, appointed to command the squadron at Basra, leading. The Rangoons arrived at Basra in mid-April and routine tasks commenced. They were joined a year later by K2134, while K2809 joined in April 1933 and K3678 in June 1934. The Rangoon continued to serve in the Middle East with 203 with no major events of note until the Short Singapore III arrived to replace the type in September 1935. Progressively, the Rangoons were sent back to the UK: S1433, S1434, S1435 and K2809 in July; and K2134 and K3678 followed in September.

The repatriation of the Rangoon to the UK was not the end of its career with the RAF. Indeed, the type found a second life with No. 210 Squadron, then based at Pembroke Dock. It converted to the Rangoons in August 1935, swapping its Singapores with 203. The squadron had a very short time to become familiar with its new aircraft as it was deployed to Gibraltar at the end of the month. They served until the end of July 1936 after which they again returned to the UK. Rangoon S1433 had already left 210 in January that year, having been sold to Imperial Airways to serve as a trainer; it would eventually be allocated the registration G-AEIM. S1433 would be the last to see service after August and all five remaining aircraft were officially struck off charge in September. During the type's short career with the RAF, none were lost, something to point at considering the reliability of the aircraft at the time and the experienced gained with both the Iris and the Perth.

Short Rangoon S1433 of 203 Squadron flying over the Persian Gulf in the mid-1930s. *(Andrew Thomas)*

Above: S1433 from the opposite side.
Below: Rangoon S1433 of 210 Squadron at Pembroke Dock before it was sent with the unit to Gibraltar.

Above: Rangoon S1435 of 210 Squadron taking off from Pembroke Dock. *(Andrew Thomas)*
Below: Rangoon K2134.

Above: Three Rangoons of 203 Squadron in front of the hangars at Basra.
Below: Rangoon K3678 of 210 Squadron at Kalafrana or Gibraltar in 1936 when the squadron was involved in carrying out security patrols during the Spanish Civil War. *(Andrew Thomas - both)*

The Short Singapore

The Short Singapore remained one of the RAF's most important seaplanes between the wars, even though it was built in small numbers (less than forty). For Shorts, it was also crucial, representing almost half of their total production of flying boats, military and civilian, in the twenty years after WWI.

The flying boat emerged at the end of WWI as an essential tool for the British Empire to help protect Britain's sea lanes and then the continued supply of advanced and high-performance seaplanes became a necessity. Short was not new in this market, having already built flying boats, like the F.3 and F.5, during the war. The study of new designs continued post-war, each time using new technology. Gathering experience, Short decided to respond to Specification 13/24, calling for an all-metal twin-engine flying boat. This was to be based, as far as Short was concerned, on its 'Cromarty', built in 1920–1921. The Short Singapore was born from that and received the serial **N179**. It was first flown on 17 August 1926. The Singapore I performed satisfactorily in the next few months and was chosen to be one of the four RAF flying boats to make a tour of Baltic ports, demonstrating the value of metal hulls. Despite this, no orders followed, mainly because the Air Ministry had, in the meantime, issued another specification – R.32/27 – calling for a long-range flying boat to be powered by three engines (Bristol Jupiter radials or Rolls-Royce Kestrel inlines). Having also built the Short Calcutta for Imperial Airways, it was logical for Short to use that design as the basis of its response to the new specification. A prototype was ordered as the Singapore Mk.II and received the serial **N246**. Structurally, the Singapore II was similar to its predecessor, but better equipped internally for self-supporting operations away from base for lengthy periods. It made its maiden flight on 27 March 1930. The first trials led to Short modifying the tail (among other things) and the single fin and rudder were changed for a triple tail unit, such as had already been adopted on the Blackburn Iris and Supermarine Southampton. Thus modified, the Singapore II flew for the first time on 17 February 1931 and started other tests, including tropical trials at Aden. Upon its return to the UK, further modifications were made which included improved radiators and oil coolers for the engines, a duralumin planing bottom on the hull and an enclosure over the cockpit. In this form, it flew on 6 May 1932 and, with some further modifications added soon after, N246 was brought virtually to the production standard defined by Specification R.3/33, against which the Air Ministry ordered four examples in August 1933. Thus, the Singapore Mk.III was finally born after many obstacles and changes of policy. The first four were serialled **K3592 to K3595** and were delivered in July (2) and November 1934 (2). They had a crew of six and were armed with three 0.303-in machine guns in nose, waist and tail positions. These four Singapores must be seen as pre-production aircraft as the following 33 airframes were all built against Specification R.14/34 which was issued for a fully developed production version with further up-rated Kestrels. Nine (**K4577–K4585**) were later ordered in 1934, followed by sixteen more in 1935 (**K6907–K6922**), and another four (**K8856–K8859**) in 1936. All were delivered between April 1935 and June 1937.

The Singapore became the epitome of pre-war RAF flying boats and led to the Sunderland which played a major role during WWII in most of the theatres of war where the RAF saw service. At the outbreak of war, nineteen Singapores were still in active service and would soldier on until the autumn of 1941 with the RAF and until the spring of 1943 with the RNZAF. The Short Singapore, while it didn't play a major role during the war, with only about 230 sorties and over 1,300 operational hours flown, was a necessary step for Shorts.

Singapore I N179. Its silhouette shows the design was mid-way between the WWI flying boats and the next generation to come. N179 is shown here in its final form with Rolls-Royce H.10 Buzzard engines and Handley Page auto-slots on the upper wings. Note the name 'Singapore' written on the bow. *(Phil Jarrett)*

Singapore Mk.II N246 was modified at various stages, starting with a new triple tail unit, that was to become the hallmark of the Singapore Mk.III, and ailerons on the lower wings (above). Afterwards, N246 was again modified with the addition of a canopy over the cockpit (see below) and improved radiators for the Kestrel engines which were also adopted as standard for the Singapore III.

No. 203 Squadron

Based at Basra (Iraq) shortly after its formation in January 1929, No. 203 Squadron operated Supermarine Southamptons and Short Rangoons before being selected to receive Singapores. Conversion began in September 1935 with the arrival of K4582 and K4583 on 24 September, while at the same time the squadron moved to Aden (Yemen) due to the invasion of Abyssinia (Ethiopia) by Mussolini's troops. By the end of the year, two other Singapores were taken on charge (K4577 and K4584) to make the full complement of four. At Aden, the main task was to fly submarine co-operation sorties as well as transporting mail. In July 1936, the squadron returned to Basra to continue more routine flights. In September, K4582 was sent to the UK and left Basra on the 15th. Seven days later, while flying the leg between Brindisi (Italy) and Berre in France, the flying boat, flown by F/L R.S. Darbyshire, was caught in a storm and obliged to make a forced landing at Paolo near Cosenza in Italy. While no injuries were reported by the crew, the Singapore could not be saved and was broken up by the waves. The following month, it was sold for scrap locally. When war broke out, the squadron moved to its war station at Aden and began anti-shipping patrols and escort work. This task began with reduced resources as two Singapores had been lost early in the year, starting with K6908 on 14 March. That day, with S/L M.Q. Candler in command, the Singapore swung while taxiing and ran aground. The flying boat was repairable but, due to its high airframe time (over 700 hours), it was decided not to conduct repairs and the aircraft was struck off charge in May. More dramatically, three weeks before the beginning of the war, the squadron lost another Singapore when, on take-off from Aboukir on 8 August, K4584, captained by S/L J.R. Scarlett-Streatfield, hit a sea wall and crashed. Among the crew, three died either that day, or the following day; it was a severe blow for the squadron just before war broke out. As already mentioned, this did not prevent the unit from beginning operations. On 4 September, F/O S.C. Pendred took off at 03.40 GMT with his crew for the first operational patrol of the war by a Singapore, followed two hours later by K6907 captained by F/O J.M.N. Pike. In September, the number of sorties rose to 22, but soon after reduced to a handful per month when it became obvious the area would not immediately be affected by the war. It was a sad state of affairs knowing the squadron was actually living its last days as a flying boat unit; before the end of the year, Blenheims began to arrive as the Singapores continued to fly anti-submarine patrols. The last of these was carried out by (now) F/L Pike with K6907 on 10 February 1940. When he landed at 20.00 that day, the squadron had performed about fifty sorties since September for 280 hours on patrol. From this moment, only No. 205 Squadron in Singapore remained operational on the type.

This photo of K4582 is believed to have been taken during the ferry flight to Iraq for service with 203 Squadron; no specific markings can be seen as the aircraft sits at its mooring. If so, it could have been taken in September 1935. *(Phil Jarrett)*

Above: an embarrassing situation for K4582 while serving with 203 Squadron at Aden. Nothing is known about the circumstances which obliged the pilot to make a forced landing on the sand. This incident is not even recorded on the aircraft's movement card, but what is clear is that it was able to be repaired to flying condition. However, the next time, returning to the UK, it ran out of luck and was unable to complete the journey, stopping in Italy.
Below: K6913 during a routine patrol while in service with 203 Squadron in Basrah (Iraq). Note the black paint covering most of the undersurfaces.

Above: K8858 just after the introduction of squadron codes in 1938 ('PP' for 203) while based at Basra. Note the individual letter 'F' was blue.
After the Munich crisis, the RAF began to camouflage its aircraft, including flying boats, and assigned squadron code letters. Stationed at Basra, 203 Squadron was assigned the letters 'NT' in September 1939. K6912 was coded 'D' within the squadron. *(Andrew Thomas)*

No. 205 Squadron

The first squadron really selected to operate the Singapore was No. 205 Squadron based at Seletar (Singapore). The first three aircraft made the journey in January 1935, arriving in April. These Singapores never returned to the UK. All were struck off charge by 1938, two (K3592 and K3593) as time-expired, the last one, K3594, after being lost in an accident at night on 2 February 1937. With S/L A.W. Bates in command, K3594 was taking off from the Johore Strait for a combined operations patrol when the flying boat swung on take-off, to avoid running aground, and a wing dug in. The Singapore crashed, causing the death of one airman, P/O R.D. Blair. Meanwhile, the squadron had received reinforcements with the arrival of K4581 in August 1935 and K6910 in May 1936. K4581 was struck off charge at the same time as the three pre-production Singapores became time-expired, while 205 continued to operate K6910, K6911 and K6916. When Britain entered the war in September 1939, things remained unchanged, except for a new CO, W/C A.F. Lang, who arrived in October. Located far from danger, as Japan wasn't yet a threat, the activities of the squadron didn't change much in the first weeks of the war. However, the squadron received reinforcements with the arrival in the spring of 1940 of another three Singapores – K6912, K6917 and K6918 – as the squadron codes 'FV' made their appearance on fuselages. Some reconnaissance flights were carried out in November 1939, mainly to locate possible German raiders. Indeed, London had asked the squadron to find and locate any German merchant vessels sailing in the area; three Singapores were not enough to successfully conduct this task. Thus, April 1940 saw a sudden increase of air activity, which reduced the following month but increased again after 10 June when Italy declared war and the squadron had to locate Italian merchant vessels. Activity reduced again in July. Nevertheless, operational activity remained at a very low level in 1939–1940 as only thirty sorties, which included some ASR flights, were recorded for a total of 175 operational flying hours. In 1941, the situation had begun to change in the region as it become clear Japan would soon enter the war. By that time, 205 was the last RAF operator of the Singapore; the type was totally obsolete by 1940 with some aircraft close to being time-expired, or actually time-expired like K6910 (struck off charge in May 1940). However, the Air Ministry had already found a successor, the Consolidated Catalina, and the first examples arrived at Seletar in April 1941. From that moment on, the Singapores flew less and less and, in October 1941, four of them (K6912, K6916, K6917 and K6918) were passed on to the Royal New Zealand Air Force (RNZAF) which needed general reconnaissance aircraft to be based on Fiji. It is unknown if the last Singapore still on charge, K6911, continued to fly after that date, but it was officially struck off charge on 11 December, three days after the beginning of the war in South-East Asia.

Singapore III K3592 while with an operational unit, 205 Squadron at Singapore. It first carried Club markings. The four allocated Singapores used the four card suits as individual identification.

Above: K3593, while serving in Singapore with 205 Squadron, with a black Spade painted under the cockpit, the first individual markings applied to the aircraft. It was painted on both sides.
Below: K6910, coded '5', over the Malayan countryside while serving with 205 Squadron in Singapore. Later, with the introduction of codes, it was allocated 'FV-F'. It was SOC on 31.05.40 for unknown reasons, either because it had reached its airframe limit or following a minor accident and not repaired, to be converted to spares to supply other Singapores still in service.

K3594 seen at various moments while serving with 205 Squadron in the Far East. First with Heart markings under the cockpit, later changed to a '7', then a '4', with which it was lost in an accident in February 1937, taking the life of one crewman.

Above: A Singapore Mk.III, coded '6', of 205 Squadron based at Seletar, below a formation of Vickers Vildebeests of 100 Squadron, in 1936. The photo doesn't allow clear identification of the Singapore involved.
Below, K6918 of 205 Squadron which had recently received camouflage and a full combination of codes, 'FV-L'. It was later transferred to the RNZAF as 'OT-D'.

No. 209 Squadron

This unit, based at Felixstowe and under the command of W/C C.R. Cox, received its first Singapore, K6909, on 13 February 1936. However, the squadron had to wait until November to receive its full complement of four machines. The squadron's task was to cover the Western Approaches and the English Channel. In 1937, under the command of W/C G.W. Bentley, the unit flew a cruise to Malta and it also co-operated in radio and radar experiments with RAF Bawdsey. Later that year, it moved to Malta for anti-piracy and anti-submarine patrols, only returning from the Mediterranean at the end of the year to begin conversion to the Stranraer. The last Singapore left the unit in December, marking the end of an uneventful two and a half years of use.

Two Singapores of 209 Squadron flying in loose formation and approaching Felixstowe in 1938, K6914/C leading, followed by K8567/M. This photo was taken from a third Singapore, K6919/Y. *(Phil Jarrett)*

An impressive photo of three Singapores of 209 Squadron in 1937. K6914/C is leading, followed by K8567/M and K6919/Y, en route to Malta for the anti-piracy mission the squadron carried out during the last three months of the year.

Singapore K6921 'Z', of 209 Squadron, setting out from Mount Batten for anti-piracy patrols in the Mediterranean, 18 September 1937. The Singapores were based at Kalafrana (Malta) for three months before returning to the UK.

K6919 served with 209 Squadron during its career and wore the letter code 'Y'. It is seen flying in line astern formation, being the last of the line, probably for a display or a ferry flight as the Singapores had no operational tactics requiring such arrangements. Note the upper wings have been repaired and the mechanics have still to repaint the roundel which has been partially cut. *(Phil Jarrett)*

No. 210 Squadron

The first unit to receive the new RAF flying boat in the UK was No. 210 Squadron based at Pembroke Dock. It was equipped at the time with the Supermarine Southampton II. The squadron was thus selected to conduct service trials and operational training with the three pre-production Singapore Mk.IIIs (K3592–K3595) in 1934. Except for K3592, all were taken on charge shortly after delivery to the RAF; K3592 was first used by the MAEE and joined the squadron after four months of trials. Once the first crews were trained, the four Singapores were sent to their overseas stations from mid-January 1935. All but one reached their destination, Singapore appropriately; K3595, captained by F/L H.L. Beatty, crashed into a hill in bad weather near Messina in Sicily on 15 February 1935. There were no survivors among the nine crewmen, including Mr. R.J. Penn from RAE Farnborough who was flying as a passenger.

Replacements for these four pre-production Singapores came in April with the arrival of the 'true' Singapores; their purpose, to train crews for the other squadrons, remained the same. K4578 was the first to arrive, followed by K4582 in June, K4583 in July, and K4584 in August but, once again, all had left for their respective units by autumn that year. In September 1935, due to the Abyssinian crisis (the invasion of Ethiopia by Italy), the squadron was temporarily equipped with Rangoons and sent to Gibraltar, returning in August 1936 to re-equip with Singapores, this time as a true operational unit. When the production of the Singapore had come to an end, the squadron was using the following aircraft: K6920, K6565, K8566, K8568, K8858 and K8859 (the last Singapore built). The number of aircraft on charge was the normal complement for an operational flying boat squadron at that time. In September 1937, the unit was detached to Algeria, as part of an Anglo–French force assembled to counter the activities of submarines attacking neutral shipping during the Spanish Civil War, and returned to the UK in December. The following year remained uneventful for the Singapores which finally left the squadron in November after 210 Squadron converted to the Short Sunderland. During most of this period, the CO of the unit had been W/C W.N. Plenderleith.

K4581 seen at Plymouth in June or July 1935 while under 210 Squadron authority before being ferried out by a crew of this unit.

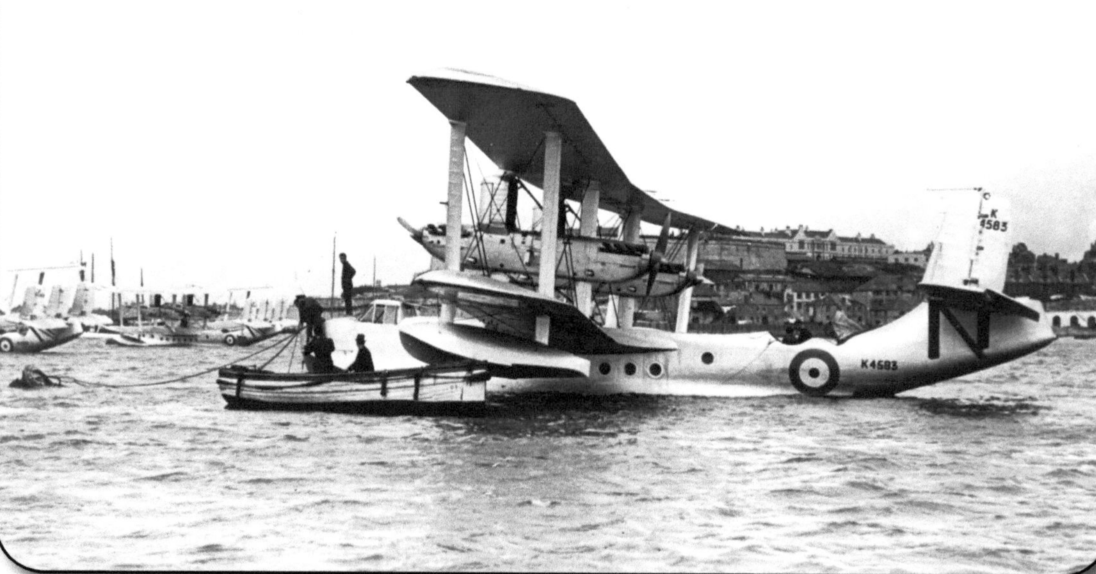

K4583 at its mooring at an unknown location, probably in the UK, just before leaving for Aden and service with 210 Squadron.

No. 230 Squadron

Starting with K4579, No. 230 Squadron began to receive its full allotment in April 1935. It was flown from the manufacturers to Pembroke Dock on the 26th. K4578 and K4580 followed in June, K4581 in July, and K4585 in August; by then the squadron had its full complement of four aircraft and one spare. In September, 230 received orders to proceed to the Middle East. The reason was for this haste was the Abyssinian crisis. Based at Alexandria, the Singapores began to undertake patrols checking on Italian shipping movements. Only one major event was recorded for this period when K4579 caught fire on start up, but the aircraft was saved from destruction due to the prompt actions of F/O Pettit and Corporal Berryman. After a year of operations, the squadron returned to the UK. The return journey came close to creating a major diplomatic issue, however, when K6912, flown by Flying Officers Oliver and Wills, had to force land off Vigo in Spain (where the Civil War had begun!). However, any incident was avoided as the crew was able to keep the engines running to avoid getting too close to the Spanish coast. A Spanish rowing boat approached but could not come alongside as K6912 was being guarded by K4580 (flown by the CO, W/C W.H. Dunn, who remained the CO during most of the Singapore era) which had landed alongside. After provisional repairs, both Singapores were able to complete the trip home. The squadron remained in the UK for a short time before leaving Pembroke Dock for Singapore in October. It stayed in the region until Short Sunderlands began to arrive in June 1938. The squadron's Singapores were handed over to No. 205 Squadron.

Two Short Singapores of 230 Squadron – K4578, coded '4', leading K4580, coded '1' – shortly after their arrival at Alexandria (Egypt) in October 1935. This photo is not representative of the flights carried out by the Singapores as they used to fly alone.

K4579 of 230 Squadron on approach to alight on the water.

Below: Singapore Mk.IIIs, including K8567 'M' and K8566 'B', of 230 Squadron being loaded onto HMS Cyclops from a jetty at Arzeu, Algeria, 1936. *(Chris Goss)*

No. 240 Squadron

This was the last squadron to be equipped with Singapores. Reformed in March 1937 by expanding C Flight of the Seaplane Training Squadron (STS) to full strength, it was originally equipped with Supermarine Scapas. However, despite this, it continued to work as a training unit until being re-equipped with Singapores in November 1938, becoming operational on 1 January 1939 under No. 16 (Coastal) Group authority with K6920, K8566 and K8568 at Calshot and S/L M.W.C. Ridgway as CO. In the next few weeks, other Singapores came to reinforce the squadron. While operational use of the Singapore was brief, about six months, 240 Squadron recorded some major accidents. The first of these occurred on 15 May 1939 when K8568, flown by F/L A.A. de Gruyther, hit the ground while descending out of cloud on return from a training flight. It force-landed at Felixstowe with a badly damaged hull. No injuries were reported by the crew but, as the Singapores were nearing the end of their service life, the aircraft was not repaired. On 6 July 1939, K6920 was wrecked. While taking off for a conversion flight, a wing dropped and a float was torn off. Nobody on board was hurt, including the pilot, P/O W.P. Green, who only had six hours on type, but the aircraft was eventually struck off charge in September for the same reasons as K8568. Despite this, Green flew throughout the war, being awarded the DSO, until he was killed in March 1945 as CO of No. 219 Squadron. Bad luck continued for 240 as, nine days later, P/O D.S.M. Burrell, with only four hours on type, did not completely control the Singapore's swing on take-off for a conversion flight and hit the mast of a steamer, damaging the aircraft. It was struck off charge before war broke out. Burrell was not lucky either as he was killed the following September while serving with No. 269 Squadron, attacking a German flying boat off Norway at the controls of an Anson. Fortunately, this run of bad luck came to an end as the Saro London had begun to arrive and the Singapores left before the end of July.

Second-line and miscellaneous units

Singapores were used by a few second-line or miscellaneous units. While an operational squadron, No. 228 Squadron's connection with the Singapore was marginal. It was re-formed as a flying boat squadron and was intended for the new Supermarine Stranraer, based at Pembroke Dock. However, the aircraft were not fully ready and the squadron had to be equipped with various spare machines, including Singapores. Even so, only three were taken on charge: K4579 between March and September 1937; K6913 between May and October 1937; and K8856 between March and July 1937. By autumn, things reverted to normal and the Stranraer became the regular equipment of the squadron. The Singapores were no longer necessary.

If we exclude the use of three Singapores (K4578, K4580, K8565) by D Flight MAEE, formally the Experimental Co-operation unit (ECU), between September 1938 and September 1939, the Singapore was principally flown by a single second-line unit, the Flying Boat Training Squadron (FBTS). Formed as part of No. 14 Group on 2 January 1939 at Calshot, it progressively took the training role of No. 240 Squadron and was equipped with various flying boats, including Singapore IIIs. Its role was to train flying boat pilots. The Singapores were sent to Calshot for FBTS use early in 1939 and, with the withdrawal of the type from front-line units, more became available and, by October 1939, K4578, K4579, K4580, K8865 and K8856 were being used to train pilots. As with many training units, the flying was not without incident and two occurred in December 1939. The first of these involved K8856 which stalled from 20 feet when landing off Hillhead (Hants). The pilot, P/O W. Beringer, didn't have a lot of experience, and only six hours on type, and was doing his first solo. The hull was damaged, although it seemed to be repairable, but the aircraft sank under tow. It was written off the following month. One week later, bad luck hit the FBTS again when P/O A.J. Bradley, while taxiing K4580 off Calshot for a practice solo flight, collided with Lerwick L7250 at its moorings. The investigation took time but, considering the pending withdrawal of the type, K4580 was struck off charge in October 1940. To make up for the attrition, K6909 arrived in December 1939. Except for its loss on 22 August 1940 when it sank in a gale, things continued without major incident until March 1941 when FBTS became the nucleus of No. 4 (C) OTU. At that time, only K4579, K6922, K8565 and K8567 remained in the inventory, soon to be joined by K4578. However, the days of the Singapores were numbered and, before June was gone, they had left the OTU.

Summary of the aircraft lost by accident after 01.09.39

Date	Pilot	S/N	Origin	Serial	Code	Unit	Fate
04.12.39	P/O William **Beringer**	RAF No. 33451	RAF	**K8856**		FBTS	-
12.12.39	P/O Arthur J. **Bradley**	RAF No. 41547	RAF	**K4580**		FBTS	-
22.08.40	*Sank in gale*	-	-	**K6909**		FBTS	-

Total: 3

SINGAPORES STILL ON RAF CHARGE AT THE OUTBREAK OF WAR

Serial	*Unit by 03.09.39*	*Final fate*
K4577	203 Sqn	SOC 04.01.40
K4578	FBTS	SOC 31.08.42
K4579	FBTS	SOC 07.05.41
K4580	FBTS	*Accident 12.12.39*
K4584	-	SOC 15.07.40 (pre-war accident damages under investigation)
K6907	203 Sqn	SOC 23.03.40
K6909	240 Sqn	*Sank in gale 22.08.40*
K6910	205 Sqn	SOC 31.05.40
K6911	205 Sqn	SOC 11.12.41
K6912	203 Sqn	To RNZAF 14.10.41
K6913	203 Sqn	SOC 20.12.40
K6916	205 Sqn	to RNZAF 14.10.41
K6917	205 Sqn	to RNZAF 14.10.41
K6918	205 Sqn	to RNZAF 14.10.41
K6922	240 Sqn	SOC 03.06.41
K8565	ECU	SOC 30.06.41
K8566	-	SOC 28.09.39 (pre-war accident damages under investigation)
K8567	240 Sqn	SOC 27.06.41
K8856	240 Sqn	*Accident 04.12.39*
K8858	203 Sqn	SOC 12.12.40
K8859	205 Sqn	SOC 20.02.41

Once withdrawn from front-line units, the Singapore helped new Coastal Command crews to train and qualify on flying boats, a task the Flying Boats Training Squadron had inherited from 240 Squadron at the outbreak of the war. The unit's denomination was later changed to No. 4 OTU. Here, K8585, coded 'Q', is seen during a training flight during the winter of 1940–1941. K8565 is wearing the standard camouflage of the period.

November 1941
January 1943

U-boat victories - confirmed or probable claims: -
Hours of patrol flown: *ca.*850

First operational sortie: 10.12.41
Last operational sortie: 23.11.42

Number of sorties: *ca.*150
Total aircraft written-off: 1
Aircraft lost on operations: -
Aircraft lost in accidents: 1

Squadron code letters:
OT

Commanding Officers

S/L Eric M. Lewis	NZ1022	RNZAF	18.11.41	05.04.42
S/L Richard J.R.H. Makgill	NZ1122	RNZAF	05.04.42	22.01.43

Squadron Usage

With Japanese intentions in South-East Asia and the Pacific becoming increasingly aggressive, the small Royal New Zealand Air Force had an urgent requirement for a flying boat to fulfil its patrol responsibilities in the South Pacific. Modern equipment, like the Catalina, was in short supply and so the RNZAF was offered some second-hand Singapores previously used by No. 205 Squadron in Singapore. Although the type was obsolescent, the Singapores were seen as a stopgap and the offer was accepted. Four aircraft – K6912, K6916, K6917 and K6918 – were allocated. Even though close to time-expired in terms of airframe hours, the

Two original Short Singapore crews, possibly at Suva (Fiji), circa 1942:
Left, the crew of Singapore K6917. Left to right, standing: Sgt E. Taylor. P/O JW Winefield, F/L W. Burgess (pilot/captain), Sgt M. Harman and LAC W. Alcock. Front: AC1 K. Kennedy and LAC S. Smart (engineer).
Right, the crew of Singapore K6916. Left to right, standing: F/Sgt E. Stuckey, S/L EM Lewis (pilot/captain), F/L R. Hickson and AC1 W. Stringer. Front, LAC F. Hughes, LAC W. Taylor and AC1 R. Gibbs.

One of the 5 Squadron Singapores under maintenance, which was also carried out by local people. Note that one crewman is adding some black paint to the hull. It is not known exactly when this Singapore received this new paint or if all were treated like this. The Singapores also received an unofficial insignia which could not be detailed with certainty but appears to be the numeral '5' with a bird and an inscription below.

Singapore K6917 being pushed into the water to carry out another patrol. Fortunately for the Kiwi crews, the area was free of Japanese fighters; the Singapore would have had little chance to escape and was easy prey for any fighters in 1942.

number of hours still to be flown were considered enough to bridge the gap before more modern and potent flying boats arrived. Before using the Singapores at the planned base on Fiji, the flying boats had to be collected. RNZAF personnel, under the responsibility of S/L E.M. Lewis, arrived at Seletar in September 1941. The New Zealanders were first trained on the type by 205 Squadron personnel and, by mid-October, the first two Singapores were ready to make the long ferry flight to Fiji. The four flying boats were officially transferred to the RNZAF on the 14th and, two days later, K6916 and K6917 lifted off from Seletar.

To operate the four Singapores, No. 5 Squadron was raised, officially formed on 18 November 1941, Lewis becoming its first CO. With tensions in South-East Asia rising, on 1 December the second ferry flight detachment in Singapore under S/L B.W. Baird was placed at the disposal of HQ Far East and logically attached to 205 Squadron. The Japanese landed on the Malayan peninsula seven days later and, during the day, the Singapores flew uneventful operational patrols. On the 10th, they provided a reconnaissance support to Force Z (HMS *Prince of Wales* and HMS *Repulse*) but had returned to base before the vessels were attacked and sunk later in the day. After these two sorties, the aircraft completed preparations at Seletar and left on the long journey to Fiji on 13 December.

In Fiji, serious operations began on 15 December when S/L Lewis flew a survey sortie in K6916 to examine proposed RDF (navigation aid) sites. However, K6916's career with the RNZAF was short as, two days later, during a take-off from Suva for a trip to Nandi captained by the CO, a creeping elevator trim became evident and the take-off was aborted. Unfortunately, the Singapore overran the surveyed alighting area and ran onto a mud bank and was severely damaged. Considering its age and the small number of spare parts and lack of facilities to undertake repairs, K6916 was declared beyond economical repair and written off in July 1942. During the month, the size of the squadron continued to be extended with the arrival of more personnel and, by the end of December, the squadron could be considered as totally operational with three Singapores, the remaining two having arrived from Seletar.

The squadron's main task was anti-submarine patrols but included convoy escorts and surface surveillance to shadow any possible Japanese surface raiders. It was also tasked with communications flights between the various islands and atolls. The first operational flight was carried out on 6 January 1942 when K6912/OT-A, captained by F/L MacGregor, flew an anti-submarine patrol. Over the next few weeks, the flights were regularly scheduled but, due to the small number of planes and spares, overall operational activity remained low, with twelve sorties in January, fifteen in February and sixteen in March. The routine continued during the next two months with an average of twenty sorties per month. The squadron added a Vickers Vincent flight on 27 May and officially became an Army Co-operation unit, but that didn't change anything for the Singapore crews. On 10 July, MacGregor and crew in K6912/OT-A provided an anti-submarine escort for the departure of the SS *Thomas Jefferson* from Suva. The crew was not long airborne before sighting a surfaced submarine, dropping a single 250-lb bomb on the rapidly submerging vessel. It was seen to go

down vertically and was claimed as damaged. That became the only claim made by a Short Singapore during the war.
At this time, the Japanese had advanced deep into the South Pacific, even appearing to threaten Fiji so, consequently, maritime reconnaissance in the area needed to be increased in importance. However, the number of Singapores and their availability did not permit this; the arrival of the US Navy's VP-11 and its Catalinas on Fiji was particularly welcomed. The squadron's former designation 'Bomber Reconnaissance' was restored during the summer but, when the unit moved to the newly completed base at Laucala Bay in September 1942, the Singapores were in decline with problems owing to age and shortage of spare parts. That month, the Singapores were able to carry out 23 sorties, but these became the swansong for the flying boat as operational activity decreased dramatically in October. It slightly increased in November, but all operational activity ceased on 23 November after F/O McHardy and crew performed the last anti-submarine patrol with K6918/OT-D. Four days later, a final flight was recorded with K6918, F/L MacGregor in command, and the squadron formally disbanded on 22 January 1943. However, due to unforeseen problems with the deployment of RNZAF Catalinas to Fiji, the Singapore Flying Boat Flight was formed under the now S/L MacGregor at Laucala Bay, in late February 1943, with two aircraft, K6912 and K6918 (K6917 having being withdrawn from use to provide spares for the other two the previous November). It was only an interim measure pending the arrival of No. 6 Squadron RNZAF with its Catalinas. Operations began on 2 March and, during the next six weeks, 22 more sorties were carried out, the last recorded on 16 April 1943. Maintenance became more difficult as the days passed, major technical problems and the chronic shortage of spares forcing the type's definitive withdrawal. The last two Singapores were eventually scuttled, marking the end of an unexpectedly long life and history of the Singapores with the RNZAF. In all, these four aircraft carried out about 175 operational sorties, representing almost 1,000 operational hours, with about 400 more hours of training and miscellaneous flights to be added to this tally. It is an impressive record considering the age of the flying boats and the various problems encountered during their service life with the RNZAF.

Summary of the aircraft lost by accident 5 Squadron RNZAF

Date	*Captain*	*S/N*	*Origin*	*Serial*	*Code*	*Fate*
17.12.41	S/L Eric M. **Lewis**	NZ1022	RNZAF	**K6916**	OT-D	-

Total: 1

The Short Singapore was totally obsolete when the British Empire entered the war against Japan in 1941. The type was a stopgap waiting for more modern aircraft, but because the war against the Japanese changed priorities regarding the delivery of aircraft, the New Zealanders had to operate the aircraft for longer than planned. Fortunately, the area they had to fly over was not an area frequented by the Japanese. Below: K6917/OT-C has just taken off for another patrol from Fiji.

Above: K6912 was transferred to the RNZAF in October 1941 and coded 'OT-A'.

Left: Singapore K6917 under major overhaul on an unspecified date, unless it was during the time it was serving as a stock of spare parts for K6912 and K6918 in 1943.

Short Singapore Mk. III K3592

No. 205 Squadron

Seletar (Singapore), 1936

Short Singapore Mk. III K3593
No. 205 Squadron
Seletar (Singapore), 1936

Short Singapore Mk. III K3593
No. 210 Squadron
Pembroke Dock (UK), 1935

Short Singapore Mk. III K3594
No. 205 Squadron
Seletar (Singapore), 1936

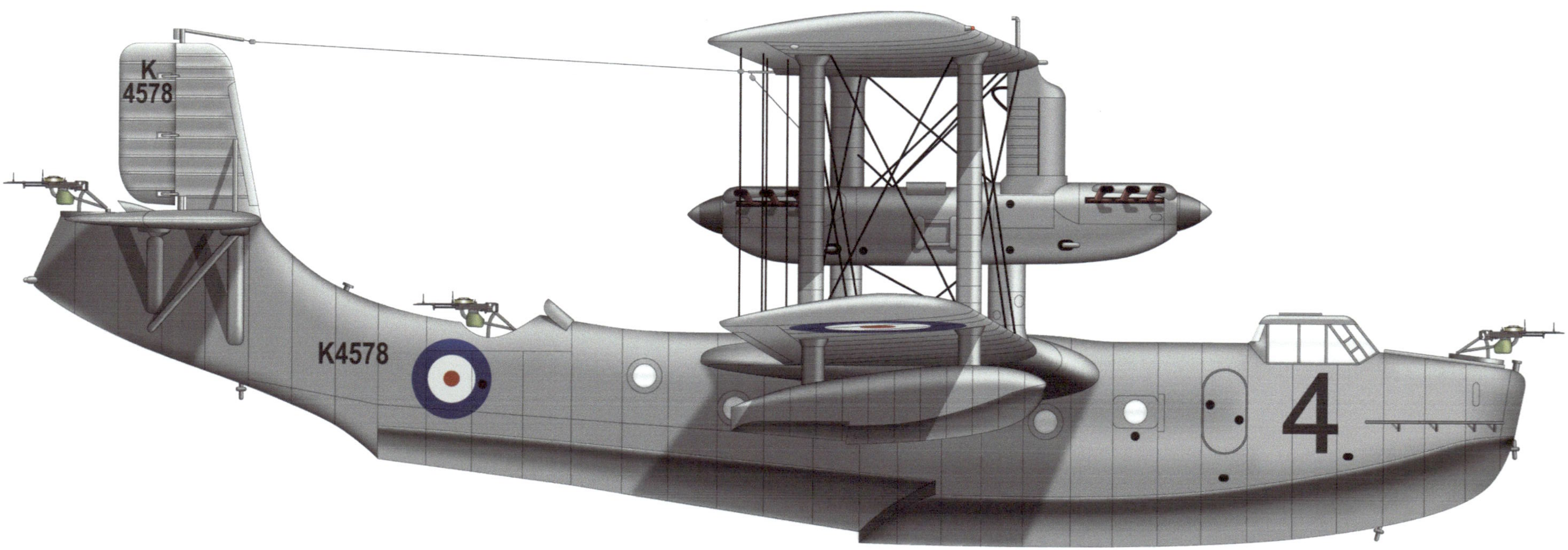

Short Singapore Mk. III K4578

No. 230 Squadron

Alexandria (Egypt), 1935

Short Singapore Mk. III K6912
No. 203 Squadron
Basra (Iraq), 1938-1939

Short Singapore Mk. III K6912
No. 5 Squadron, RNZAF
Fiji, 1942

Short Singapore Mk. III K6913

No. 203 Squadron

Basra (Iraq), 1938

Short Singapore Mk. III K6918
No. 203 Squadron
Seletar (Sinpagore), spring 1941

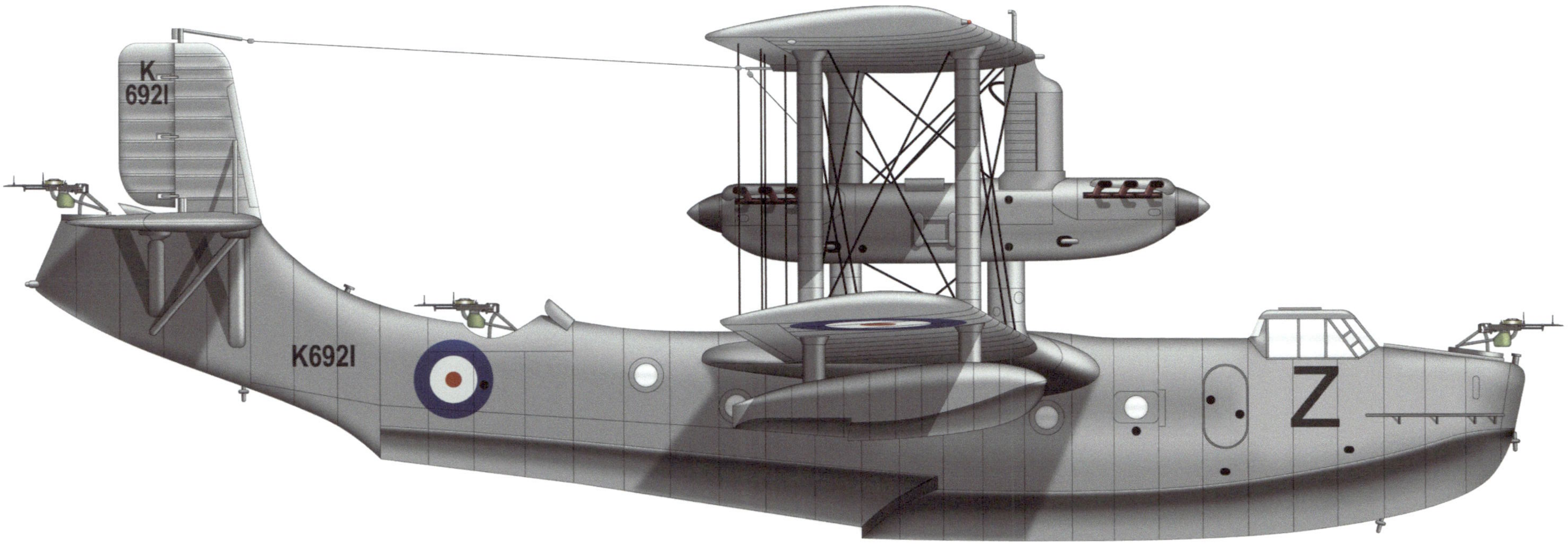

Short Singapore Mk. III K6921
No. 209 Squadron
Mountbatten (UK), autumn 1937

Short Singapore Mk. III K8565
No. 4 (C) OTU
Stranraer (UK), 1940-1941

Short Singapore Mk. III K8858
No. 203 Squadron
Basra (Iraq), 1938

SQUADRONS! - The series

1 The Supermarine Spitfire Mk VI
2 The Republic Thunderbolt Mk I
3 The Supermarine Spitfire Mk V in the Far East
4 The Boeing Fortress Mk I
5 The Supermarine Spitfire Mk XII
6 The Supermarine Spitfire Mk VII
7 The Supermarine Spitfire F. 21
8 The Handley-Page Halifax Mk I
9 The Forgotten Fighters
10 The NA Mustang IV in Western Europe
11 The NA Mustang IV over the Balkans and Italy
12 The Supermarine Spitfire Mk XVI - The British
13 The Martin Marauder Mk I
14 The Supermarine Spitfire Mk VIII in the Southwest Pacific- The British
15 The Gloster Meteor F.I & F.III
16 The NA Mitchell - The Dutch, Poles and French
17 The Curtiss Mohawk
18 The Curtiss Kittyhawk Mk II
19 The Boulton Paul Defiant - day and night fighter
20 The Supermarine Spitfire Mk VIII in the Southwest Pacific - The Australians
21 The Boeing Fortress Mk II & Mk III
22 The Douglas Boston and Havoc - The Australians
23 The Republic Thunderbolt Mk II
24 The Douglas Boston and Havoc - Night fighters
25 The Supermarine Spitfire Mk V - The Eagles
26 The Hawker Hurricane - The Canadians
27 The Supermarine Spitfire Mk V - The 'Bombay' squadrons
28 The Consolidated Liberator - The Australians
29 The Supermarine Spitfire Mk XVI - The Dominions
30 The Supermarine Spitfire Mk V - The Belgian and Dutch squadrons
31 The Supermarine Spitfire Mk V - The New Zealanders
32 The Supermarine Spitfire Mk V - The Norwegians
33 The Brewster Buffalo
34 The Supermarine Spitfire Mk II - The Foreign squadrons
35 The Martin Marauder Mk II
36 The Supermarine Spitfire Mk V - The Special Reserve squadrons
37 The Supermarine Spitfire Mk XIV - The Belgian and Dutch squadrons
38 The Supermarine Spitfire Mk II - The Rhodesian, Dominion & Eagle squadrons
39 The Douglas Boston and Havoc - Intruders
40 The North American Mustang Mk III over Italy and the Balkans (Pt-1)
41 The Bristol Brigand
42 The Supermarine Spitfire Mk V - The Australians
43 The Hawker Typhoon - The Rhodesian squadrons
44 The Supermarine Spitfire F.22 & F.24
45 The Supermarine Spitfire Mk IX - The Belgian and Dutch squadrons
46 The North American & CAC Mustang - The RAAF
47 The Westland Whirlwind
48 The Supermarine Spitfire Mk XIV - The British squadrons
49 The Supermarine Spitfire Mk I - The beginning (the Auxiliary squadrons)
50 The Hawker Tempest Mk V - The New Zealanders
51 The Last of the Long-Range Biplane Flying Boats
52 The Supermarine Spitfire Mk IX - The Former Canadian Homefront squadrons
53 The Hawker Hurricane Mk I & Mk II - The Eagle squadrons
54 The Hawker biplane fighters
55 The Supermarine Spitfire Mk IX - The Auxiliary squadrons
56 The Hawker Typhoon - The Canadian squadrons

The Supermarine SPITFIRE Mk.V in the Far East
No.3
USN AIRCRAFT 1922-1962
Vol.7: Type Designation Letter 'F' (Pt-4)
Phil H. LISTEMANN
RAF, Dominion & Allied Squadrons at War: Study, History and Statistics
No.137 Squadron 1941 - 1945
Compiled by
Phil H. Listemann with Chris Thomas
Fighter Leaders
Volume VII
Phil H. Listemann
No.10
The North American Mustang Mk. IV in Western Europe
www.RAF-IN-COMBAT.com
- USN Aircraft 1922-1962 -
- Squadrons! -
- RAF, Dominion and Allied squadrons at War -
- Allied Wings -
- Famous squadrons of WW2 -
- Fighter Leaders -
RAF, Dominion & Allied Squadron at War: Study, History and Statistics
No.131 (County of Kent) Squadron 1941 - 1945
Famous Commonwealth Squadrons of WW2
No.453 (R.A.A.F.) Squadron 1941-1945 Buffalo, Spitfire
Allied Wings
Squadrons!
The Bristol Brigand

www.ingramcontent.com/pod-product-compliance
Ingram Content Group UK Ltd.
Pitfield, Milton Keynes, MK11 3LW, UK
UKHW060121300726
14090UKWH00002B/299

* 9 7 9 1 0 9 6 4 9 0 8 6 8 *